Isis

BY VIRGINIA LOH-HAGAN

Gods and goddesses were the main characters of myths. Myths are traditional stories from ancient cultures. Storytellers answered questions about the world by creating exciting explanations. People thought myths were true. Myths explained the unexplainable. They helped people make sense of human behavior and nature. Today, we use science to explain the world. But people still love myths. Myths may not be literally true. But they have meaning. They tell us something about our history and culture.

45th Parallel Press

Published in the United States of America by Cherry Lake Publishing
Ann Arbor, Michigan
www.cherrylakepublishing.com

Reading Adviser: Marla Conn, MS, Ed., Literacy specialist, Read-Ability, Inc.
Book Design: Jen Wahi

Photo Credits: ©Howard David Johnson, 2019, cover, 1, 19; ©TerryJLawrence/iStock, 5; Internet Archive Book Images/
flickr/Public domain, 6; Leon Jean Joseph Dubois (1780–1846)/rawpixel/Public domain, 9; ©Catmando/Shutterstock, 11;
Jebulon, photographer/Wikimedia/Public domain, 13; ©GNT STUDIO/Shutterstock, 14; ©Orhan Cam/Shutterstock, 17;
©Milan Zygmunt/Shutterstock, 21; ©Vladimir Melnik /Shutterstock, 23; ©Anton Calpagiu/Shutterstock, 24; ©Alberto Loyo/
Shutterstock, 27; ©Morphart Creation/Shutterstock, 29

45th Parallel Press is an imprint of Cherry Lake Publishing.

Library of Congress Cataloging-in-Publication Data

Names: Loh-Hagan, Virginia, author. | Loh-Hagan, Virginia. Gods & goddesses of the ancient world.
Title: Isis / written by Virginia Loh-Hagan.
Description: Ann Arbor, Michigan : Cherry Lake Publishing, 2019. | Series: Gods and goddesses of the ancient world |
    Includes bibliographical references and index.
Identifiers: LCCN 2019004186 | ISBN 9781534147751 (hardcover) | ISBN 9781534149182 (pdf) | ISBN 9781534150614 (pbk.) |
    ISBN 9781534152045 (hosted ebook)
Subjects: LCSH: Isis (Egyptian deity)—Juvenile literature. | Goddesses, Egyptian—Juvenile literature. | Mythology, Egyptian—
    Juvenile literature.
Classification: LCC BL2450.I7 L64 2019 | DDC 299/.312114—dc23
LC record available at https://lccn.loc.gov/2019004186

Printed in the United States of America
Corporate Graphics

ABOUT THE AUTHOR:

Dr. Virginia Loh-Hagan is an author, university professor, former classroom teacher, and curriculum designer. Like Isis, she is very protective. Her dogs are her children. She lives in San Diego with her very tall husband and very naughty dogs. To learn more about her, visit www.virginialoh.com.

TABLE OF CONTENTS

ABOUT THE AUTHOR 2

CHAPTER 1:
A TRICKY BIRTH 4

CHAPTER 2:
FAMILY FEUD 10

CHAPTER 3:
A MOTHER'S LOVE 16

CHAPTER 4:
SEEING STARS 22

CHAPTER 5:
NOT JUST A PRETTY FACE 26

DID YOU KNOW? 30
CONSIDER THIS! 31
LEARN MORE 31
GLOSSARY 32
INDEX 32

A TRICKY BIRTH

Who is Isis? What does she look like? How is she born?

Isis was an **ancient** Egyptian goddess. Ancient means old. Egypt is a country in the Middle East. It's in North Africa.

Ancient Egyptians honored Isis. Isis was the goddess of marriage. She was the goddess of **fertility**. Fertility means the ability to reproduce or grow. Isis was the goddess of motherhood. She was the goddess of magic. She was the goddess of medicine.

Isis was beautiful. She took human form. She wore a **headdress**. A headdress is a fancy head covering.

Her headdress looked like a bird on its stomach. The bird rested on top of Isis's head. Its head hung over her forehead. Its wings hung down the sides of her head. Isis often wore wings on her arms.

Sometimes Isis wears a crown. The crown has horns. It has a sun disc.

Ennead comes from the Greek word for "nine." Pictured are 4 of the 9 Ennead and a guard.

Isis was a member of the Great Ennead. The Ennead were the 9 most important gods and goddesses. They were the original gods and goddesses of ancient Egypt.

Isis was born soon after the creation of the world. Her parents were Nut and Geb. Nut was the goddess of the sky. Geb was the god of the earth. They were in love. Ra was Nut and Geb's grandfather. He was the god of the sun.

He was worried about losing his power. He didn't want Nut and Geb to have children. He made a command. He said, "Nut isn't allowed to give birth any day of the year."

Family Tree

Grandparents: Shu (god of light and dry air) and Tefnut (goddess of wet air and rain)

Parents: Geb (god of the earth) and Nut (goddess of the sky)

Brothers: Osiris (god of the dead and rebirth) and Set (god of disorder and deserts)

Sister: Nephthys (goddess of darkness and water)

Spouse: Osiris (god of the afterlife, underworld, and rebirth)

Child: Horus (god of the sky, kings, and war)

Adopted Child: Anubis (god of embalming)

Nut went to Thoth. Thoth was the god of wisdom. Nut and Thoth came up with a plan. Thoth tricked Khonsu. Khonsu was the god of the moon. Thoth played a game with Khonsu. Every time Khonsu lost, he had to give some of his light to Thoth. Khonsu lost many times. Thoth had enough moonlight to make 5 extra days. These days were not part of the year.

So, Nut was able to give birth. She had 4 children with Geb. Her children were Osiris, Set, Nephthys, and Isis. They managed all human matters on earth. They also created all the other gods of Egypt.

 Nut was the sky goddess. Her body arched over the earth.

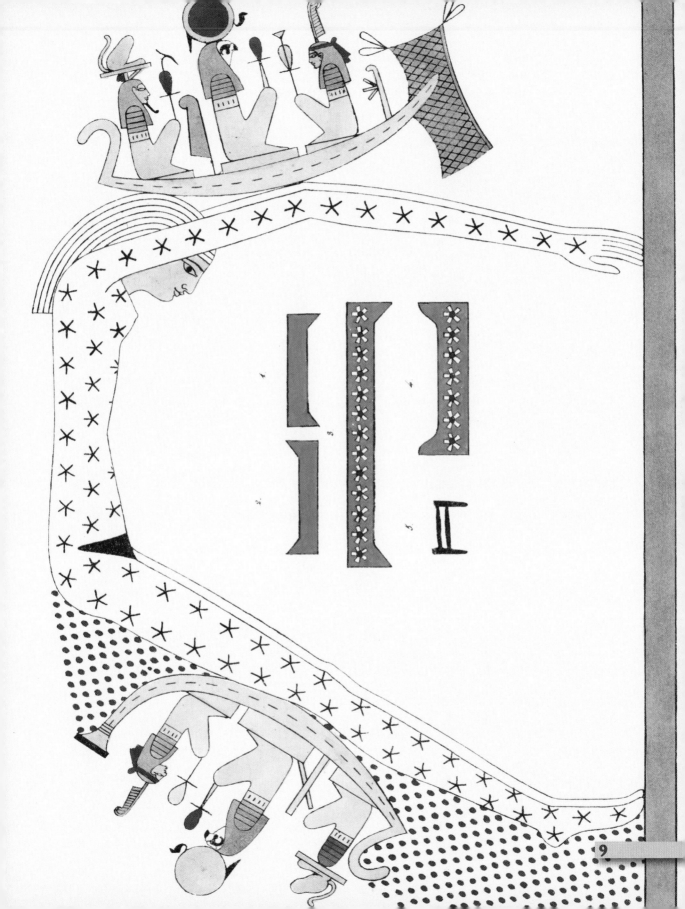

CHAPTER 2

FAMILY FEUD

Who does Isis marry? How does Isis help humans? How does Isis save her husband?

The ancient Egyptian gods married their own family members. For example, Isis's parents were also brother and sister. Ancient Egyptians married their own family members too. They did this to keep royal blood in the family. Royal means related to kings and queens.

Isis followed her mother's footsteps. She married her brother, Osiris. Isis and Osiris loved each other. Osiris ruled the world. Isis became his queen. Together, they created a nice world for humans. They taught humans how to farm and fish.

They told humans to get married and have children. Isis taught women how to weave and cook. She protected the sea. She wanted families to stay together.

Their brother, Set, was jealous. He wanted power. He tricked Osiris. He made a **coffin** for Osiris. Coffins are cases that hold dead bodies. Set threw a party. He brought out the

Sailors wore necklaces with Isis's pictures. They prayed to her for safe travels.

All in the Family

Nut was the goddess of the sky. She's also known as the mother of all gods. Her grandfather was Ra. Ra was a powerful god. He was the god of the sun. Every night, Nut ate Ra. Then, she gave birth to Ra every morning. This was how each day was created. Nut married her brother, Geb. Nut lived in the sky. Geb lived on earth. Nut and Geb were apart during the day. At night, Nut came down to earth to be with Geb. The night is dark because Nut was not in the sky. Nut and Geb loved each other a lot. They were always hugging. Nut's father, Shu, was air. He separated Nut and Geb. This was why the sky is separated from the earth. Nut gave birth to all the stars and planets. She also had four children: Osiris, Set, Isis, and Nephythys.

During her searches, Isis would dress like an old woman.

coffin. He dared people to get in. Osiris liked games. He got in. Set shut the coffin. He threw it in the Nile River.

Isis was very sad. She searched for Osiris all over Egypt. She couldn't find him.

Osiris floated to sea. He got trapped in a big tree. The tree grew around his coffin. A king cut down the tree. He used

it as a **pillar** for his castle. Pillars are like tall posts. Osiris was in the pillar. He died trapped inside.

Isis searched the Nile River. She cried and cried. She flooded the river with her tears.

The king found Isis. He brought her back to his castle. Isis admired the pillar. She asked if she could have it. She found Osiris's dead body inside.

Set found out. He hacked Osiris's body into many pieces. He scattered his body parts all over. Isis became a bird. She found most of Osiris's body parts. She used magic. She brought Osiris back to life. This made her famous. Isis was known for her healing powers. People said she was "more powerful than a thousand soldiers."

 Isis went to the Nile River every year. She cried remembering her sadness.

CHAPTER 3

A MOTHER'S LOVE

How does Isis rule the dead? How is Isis a good mother?

Osiris now lived. But he wasn't the same. He was both alive and dead. He became the god of the **underworld**. The underworld is where the dead live. Set took over the world of the living.

Isis stood by Osiris. She joined him in the underworld. She protected the dead. She fought against evil.

Ancient Egyptians thought royal bodies should be saved. They turned dead bodies into **mummies**. Mummies are wrapped bodies. People's organs were taken out of their bodies. These organs were saved in special jars. The jars were protected by a god or goddess. The god or goddess was also protected by another god or goddess.

Imset, son of Horus, watched over the jar of livers. Isis watched over Imset. Isis helped people get to the **afterlife**. Afterlife is what happens after death.

Isis is depicted on many ancient coffins.

Isis took on whatever role she needed. She now wanted to be a mother. She used her magic. She became a bird. She flew around Osiris. Then, she gave birth to their son. The son's name was Horus.

Horus was born to seek **revenge**. Revenge means to get even. But Isis had to protect Horus from Set. She hid him by the Nile River. She took care of him. Horus grew up. He fought Set. He took back his father's throne. He ruled with Isis by his side. He became the symbol for **pharaohs**. Pharaohs are the rulers of ancient Egypt. Isis became known as the mother of pharaohs.

Isis helped Horus. She used her magic to help him win battles. In some stories, it's believed she felt bad for Set. She didn't help Horus. Horus got mad. He cut off her head.

Isis is compared to the Virgin Mary, a divine figure in Christianity.

Real World Connection

In 2014, 399 female babies in the United States were named Isis. But today, being named Isis can be confusing. ISIS refers to the Islamic State of Iraq and Syria. This is a powerful group. They're terrorists. Terrorists use violence. ISIS has taken control over large areas in the Middle East. They plan attacks. They kill. They bomb. Women named Isis don't want to be connected to ISIS. Some people started an online petition. Petitions are formal requests. The petition states, "Help us take back our name." These women want the media to use another name to describe the terrorist group. They have suffered because of the connection. There was a technology company named Isis. It changed its name. The head of the company said, "We have no desire to share a name with this group. And our hearts go out to those affected by this violence."

In one story, Set sent a scorpion to sting Horus. Horus was a baby. Isis saved him.

But Isis used magic to grow a cow's head. She also forgave Horus.

Isis was a good mother. She protected Horus no matter what. She also protected other mothers' children. One day, Isis was dressed like an old woman. She asked a rich woman for help. The rich woman turned her away. This made the scorpion goddesses angry. They stung the rich woman's son. The rich woman didn't want her son to die. Isis helped. She healed her son. She forgave the rich woman.

CHAPTER 4

SEEING STARS

What are Isis's symbols?

Isis had many symbols. Her animals were cows, snakes, and scorpions. Isis's birds were doves, hawks, swallows, and vultures. In several stories, she turned into a **kite**. Kites are birds of prey. They're hunters. They're **scavengers**. Scavengers eat dead bodies.

Isis had a long **staff**. A staff is like a pole. It had an animal head on top. It had magical powers. Isis also had an **ankh**. An ankh is shaped like a cross with an open top. It represents eternal life. Eternal means forever.

The **tyet** is known as the knot of Isis. A tyet looks like an ankh but with the arms down. It represents life. It's often colored in red. Knots also mean magic.

Isis liked scorpions. The seven scorpion goddesses protected Isis. They kept her safe when she was hiding with Horus.

Ancient Egyptians didn't bury their dead during the 70 days that Sirius was hidden from view. This meant the doorway to the afterlife was closed.

Isis is connected to a very special star. **Sirius** is the brightest star in the sky. It's called the Dog Star. The ancient Egyptians called it the Star of Isis. Some called it the Nile Star.

Around June, ancient Egyptians watched Isis's temple. A statue of Isis was in the temple. It was placed to mark the rising of Sirius. A jewel was put on Isis's forehead. Sirius's light would hit the gem. This was how ancient Egyptians knew the new year was coming. Ancient Egyptians saw

Sirius rising just before the sun. They knew this meant the Nile River was going to flood.

Some people think that the rising of Sirius was connected to Horus's birth.

Cross-Cultural Connection

Matrika means godly mother. Matrikas are mother goddesses. They're sometimes called the "ancient mothers." There are 7 to 8 matrikas. They're always together. They represent ideas like desire, anger, greed, pride, and envy. They're part of the Hindu religion. Hinduism is the largest religion in India. About 80 percent of Indians are Hindus. The matrikas help fight demons. But they can also be dangerous. They're known to kidnap and eat children. When young children die, the matrikas are to blame. People worship them to keep evil away. The matrikas also do good things. They protect children. They nurse children. They help mothers have babies. They give powers to fight enemies.

CHAPTER 5

NOT JUST A PRETTY FACE

How is Isis tricky? How does she get more powers?

Isis had it all. She was powerful. She was smart. But she wanted more. She wanted Ra's power. There was only one way to get his power. Isis needed Ra's secret name.

Ra became an old man. He drooled a lot. He was walking across the heavens. His spit fell to the earth. Isis took Ra's spit. She mixed it with dirt. She made a snake. She didn't need her magic. Ra's spit was powerful enough.

Isis put the snake in Ra's path. The snake bit Ra. Ra felt death. He asked Isis for help. Isis said, "I'll heal you. I'll kill the snake. But you have to tell me your secret name."

Ra didn't want to. But he gave in. He felt the poison in his body. He told Isis his secret name. Isis did as she promised.

The great hooded snake is the symbol of all goddesses.

Explained By Science

The Nile River used to flood. This happened every summer from June to September. This happened for thousands of years. The flood made land good for farming. Farming gave people food. Ancient Egyptians had 3 stages of the flood cycle. The first was the flooding time. The second was the planting time. The third was the harvesting time. This cycle kept Egyptians from dying of hunger. Ancient Egyptians thought the Nile River flooded because of Isis's tears for her dead husband. Science has a different story. Winds from the northern and southern parts of the world flew into the Ethiopian mountains. Wet air from the Indian Ocean rose. This created rain. Melting snow and rains from the Ethiopian mountains sent a lot of water into the banks of the Nile River. This caused the Nile to flood. Water overflowed onto flat desert land. The Aswan Dam was finished in 1971. Dams block water. Now, the flooding is controlled.

In some stories, Isis is thought to be Hapi's wife.

Then, she took his powers. She made Horus the king of the gods. She also gave herself more magical powers.

Don't anger the goddesses. Isis had great powers. And she knew how to use them.

DID YOU KNOW?

- Isis's Egyptian name is Iset or Aset. Isis is actually an ancient Greek name. It is a Greek word for "throne." Thrones are special chairs for rulers.

- Isis was worshipped all over the Roman Empire. She was worshipped from England to Afghanistan. Some people still worship Isis today. People who worship her are called the "cult of Isis." Cults are special groups.

- People built several temples to Isis. Temples are buildings designed to honor gods. Isis has temples in Alexandria. Alexandria is a big city in Egypt. It's by the sea. In Alexandria, people thought Isis protected sailors.

- Ancient Greeks conquered Egypt around 332 BCE. They connected Isis to Demeter. Demeter was a popular ancient Greek goddess. This connection made it easy for ancient Greeks to worship Isis.

- Ancient Romans connected Isis to Ceres and Venus. Ceres was the Roman goddess of farming and motherhood. Venus was the Roman goddess of love and fertility.

- Cleopatra was queen of ancient Egypt. She ruled for about 30 years. She was the last true pharaoh of Egypt. She connected herself to Isis. She liked being called the New Isis. She dressed like Isis. She was a mother like Isis. She had a son. She protected her son.

- There was an ancient festival for Isis. Festivals are like parties. Isis's festival celebrated her power over the sea. People prayed for the safety of sailors. People marched in parades. They dressed in fancy clothes. They carried a toy ship from Isis's temple to the sea.

CONSIDER THIS!

TAKE A POSITION! Read the 45th Parallel Press book about Osiris. Who is more powerful: Isis or Osiris? Argue your point with reasons and evidence.

SAY WHAT? Read 45th Parallel Press books about Greek and Roman goddesses. Which goddess is Isis most like? Explain how the goddesses are alike. Explain how they're different.

THINK ABOUT IT! Isis has the power of healing. How did she use this power? Imagine if you had this power. What would you do with it?

LEARN MORE

Limke, Jeff, and David Witt (illust.). *Isis & Osiris: To the Ends of the Earth.* Minneapolis, MN: Graphic Universe, 2007.

Maurer, Gretchen. *Call Me Isis: Egyptian Goddess of Magic.* Foster City, CA: Goosebottom Books, 2014.

Napoli, Donna Jo, and Christina Balit (illust.). *Treasury of Egyptian Mythology: Classic Stories of Gods, Goddesses, Monsters, and Mortals.* Washington, DC: National Geographic Kids, 2013.

GLOSSARY

afterlife (AF-tur-life) the time after death

ancient (AYN-shuhnt) old, from a long time ago

ankh (ANK) an object with a loop used in ancient Egypt as a symbol of life

coffin (KAW-fin) a case that holds a dead body

fertility (fur-TIL-ih-tee) the ability to reproduce or grow

headdress (HED-dres) a fancy, ornamental head covering usually decorated with symbols

kite (KITE) a type of bird of prey

mummies (MUHM-eez) wrapped bodies that are being preserved over time

pharaohs (FAIR-ohz) ancient Egyptian rulers

pillar (PIL-ur) column or large pole

revenge (rih-VENJ) the act of getting even

scavengers (SKAV-uhn-jurz) beings that eat dead bodies

Sirius (SEER-ee-uhs) brightest star in the sky

staff (STAF) a long pole used as support when walking or climbing or as a weapon or held as a sign of power

tyet (TYE-it) symbol meaning the knot of Isis

underworld (UHN-dur-wurld) the land of the dead

INDEX

A
afterlife, 17, 24

E
Egypt, 4, 30

G
Geb, 6–8, 12

H
Horus, 18, 21, 23, 25, 29

I
Isis, 20, 30
    family, 6–8, 10, 12
    how she rules the dead, 16–17
    how she's tricky, 26–29
    husband (See Osiris)
    as mother, 21
    symbols of, 22–25
    what she looked like, 4–5
    who she is, 4–9

K
Khonsu, 8

N
Nile River, 15, 18, 25, 28
Nut, 6–8, 12

O
Osiris, 7, 10–11, 13, 15, 16, 18

R
Ra, 6–8, 12, 26–29

S
Set, 11–12, 13, 15, 16, 18, 21
Sirius, 24–25

T
Thoth, 8

U
underworld, 16